CATH KIDSTON
VINTAGE STYLE

CREATING A COMPLETE LOOK FOR YOUR HOME

CATH KIDSTON
VINTAGE STYLE

PHOTOGRAPHS   PIA TRYDE

A Bulfinch Press Book
Little, Brown and Company
Boston   New York   London

To my family

First North American Edition

First published in the United Kingdom in 1999 by Ebury Press
Random House, 20 Vauxhall Bridge Road, London SW1V 2SA

ISBN 0-8212-2602-9

Library of Congress Catalog Card Number 99-073268

DESIGNED BY **GEORGINA RHODES**

Bulfinch Press is an imprint and trademark of Little, Brown and Company (Inc.)

PRINTED IN SINGAPORE

introduction

RIGHT

At home. By chance
I am dressed to match
my pink and white
sitting room!

My fascination with interior design began at a very early age. For some strange reason I can recollect every inch of my childhood home, my best friend's bedroom curtains, or the color of a certain armchair. While I am hopeless at remembering all sorts of important things, such as telephone numbers or shopping lists, I can recollect an exact fabric or wallpaper that I may not have seen for fifteen years. I am not quite sure how my obsession began.

While both my parents were very interested in the decoration of our house and took a good deal of trouble in making it pretty, once they had furnished the rooms and hung the curtains, they let the place be. The emphasis was very much on it being a comfortable family home with the dogs allowed to sit on the sofa and even our donkey coming into the sitting room for tea and chocolate cookies. It was not consciously a haven of interior design.

Early experiments

I probably spent most of my childhood outdoors on a pony, but the thing I remember most is the excitement of choosing my own curtains for the first time and the fun I had constantly rearranging my bedroom furniture. Since then I have spent quite a few years involved in interior design.

I have seen all sorts of trends come and go; from stripped pine and peach stippled walls to grand swags and tails. My own taste has changed and adapted over this time, but somehow the thing that has most influenced me and I have repeatedly come back to are the prints and fabrics of my childhood. I was contemplating this one day as I sat at home wading through piles of old books and magazines. I wanted to start my own interior design shop at the time but needed some sort of push to give me the confidence to do so. I felt there had to be a way of combining these old designs into contemporary decorating. The bold cabbage rose curtains I had kept all those years or that lilac chintz I had found at auction looked far fresher to me than anything that was on the market. Then I came across the most wonderful photograph of a bathroom. It was a complete inspiration to me. The walls were the palest duck egg blue paint, the floor plain cork tiling. The furniture was simple and practical, too. A large laundry cupboard on the back wall, a simple table and chair by the bath – and all painted shiny white. A set of classic Redouté rose prints hung on the wall and a sheepskin mat lay by the bath. But what made the room was the completely unexpected, rather eccentric, splash of cabbage rose wallpaper covering the panels

of the bath. This room must have been decorated about thirty years ago and yet it had a freshness, originality and honesty about it that is hard to find today.

Creating my shop

Inspired by this photograph I set about starting my own business. The first thing I did was to invest half of my minuscule budget in developing my own cabbage print wallpaper. I chose classic red roses with dark green leaves on a fresh white background, just like the panel around the old bath tub. I then combed the junk shops and markets for furniture and vintage fabrics.

I was encouraged at how easy it was to find handsome pieces of furniture for very little money. Most of them needed a coat of paint, but were easily transformed. The wallpaper was perfect for lining the cupboards and drawers and it is amazing what a difference a new set of handles can make.

The biggest surprise of all, though, was the availability of the old fabrics. I wasn't interested in grand silk damask or French toile de Jouy – instead, I focused on finding the cheerful floral prints of my childhood. It was simply a question of rummaging around at flea markets or sale rooms rather than going to smart antique shops, but there was plenty to be found.

LEFT

An old eiderdown gets a new lease of life with a paisely loose cover. The edges are trimmed in taffetta, an idea copied from the original quilt.

OPPOSITE

The colors of this oil painting inspired the color scheme for my bedroom.

RIGHT

*I bought these
wire shelves from
a garage sale with no
particular use
in mind. But they
have worked out as
ideal storage for
the stationery in
my office.*

The thing that had struck me most about the bathroom picture had been the unexpected use of the floral paper on the side of the bath. The element of surprise appealed to me in particular and triggered my imagination. I loved the idea of using my favorite old chintz for a laundry bag instead of curtain, or that leftover piece of striped linen for perhaps a roller towel.

So I started to turn these ideas into products for my shop. Ironing board covers made from lengths of vintage dress fabric were the first experiment, and I was so encouraged by their popularity that other items soon followed.

Decorating my home

Around this time I moved house and it was the perfect opportunity to experiment with these ideas at home. I painted the entire place white from top to toe in order to move in with a clean slate and slowly began the decorating.

I have gathered quite a lot of furniture and pictures over the years and many of these objects are of great sentimental value. Some things I collected a while ago and are no longer fashionable but I wanted to try and use most of what I had. It turned out that this actually helped rather than restrained the decorating. For example, a bright pink and yellow oil painting by my great aunt inspired the colors for my sitting room, and an old skipping rope with red and torquoise paint gave me the idea of adding blue to my red and white kitchen. The color scheme of my lilac and green bedroom also stemmed from some paintings I had inherited.

Once I had decided on the basic idea for each room I could begin to decorate. For instance, in my kitchen I felt safe with the idea of ordering a bright blue stove and knew that I could then collect fabrics for tablecloths, seat cushions and even the tea towels. Gradually I began to build each room, buying things as I came across them in junk stores and markets. Several years have now passed and although the house has had a lived-in feel for some time, the decoration continues to evolve. I still love combing the junk stores and markets and never know what I will find next. Also, as I now have a much wider collection of my own fabrics and wallpapers in my shop, I can use these at home. I love to combine them with the old fabrics and there is nothing like finding a wonderful old pair of rosy curtains at a garage sale.

This book is really an illustration of how, with my love of textiles and everday household objects, I have developed a certain style of decorating. I am sure my taste will change again with time, but my love of floral chintz will always remain.

the kitchen

the kitchen

The kitchen really is the heart of our house. More time is spent chatting around the kitchen table than anywhere else and besides cooking and eating it is used as the main congregating area throughout the day for the family. In London we have opened up the entire basement area to form a large kitchen. The cooking is at one end, the table in the middle and a sitting area with a fireplace and television at the far end. At first glance, this is a fantastic room, but in practice it has many drawbacks. We seem to spend our entire time in the basement, which is rather dark, and never use our living room on the ground floor. Added to this, the room is also used as a playroom, so it is forever strewn with toys, newspapers and clutter. When we bought our house in the country I made sure we arranged the living space in a much more segregated way and now we spread ourselves throughout the house.

Before we moved in I painted the entire interior white in order to start with a clean slate. I didn't want to make any hurried decisions and as time goes by I am gradually painting a few of the rooms in different colors. Much of the house will remain white, the kitchen in particular, as I like the versatility that this gives me in decorating the rest of the room. After the dark basement kitchen, I wanted to keep the new one as light as possible and I didn't want to use a color that would be tying in years to come. Kitchens are the one room in the house that need to be repainted fairly regularly, so it also seemed the most practical solution as it is simple to add a fresh coat of white paint. The only thing that guided me in choosing the other colors for the room was that over the years I have collected an enormous amount of red and white kitchenware. There is everything from striped storage jars to checkered enamel pans, egg cups, soup ladles and mugs. I knew I wanted to use this all again but I also wanted a change from my previous red and white kitchen so have introduced blue as well. Once I had decided on these colors, the basis of the room was set.

Making changes

First of all I was lucky enough to find a new cooker that was available in a wonderful blue enamel. It heats up in the same way as an old-fashioned range to keep the kitchen cosy in the winter and is the focal point of the room. A plain chimney breast was then built around the stove with a simple mantel shelf over the top to disguise the hood. To complete the space, I then tiled behind the stove with plain white tiles.

We had inherited kitchen cupboards and I was loathe to throw them all away as they

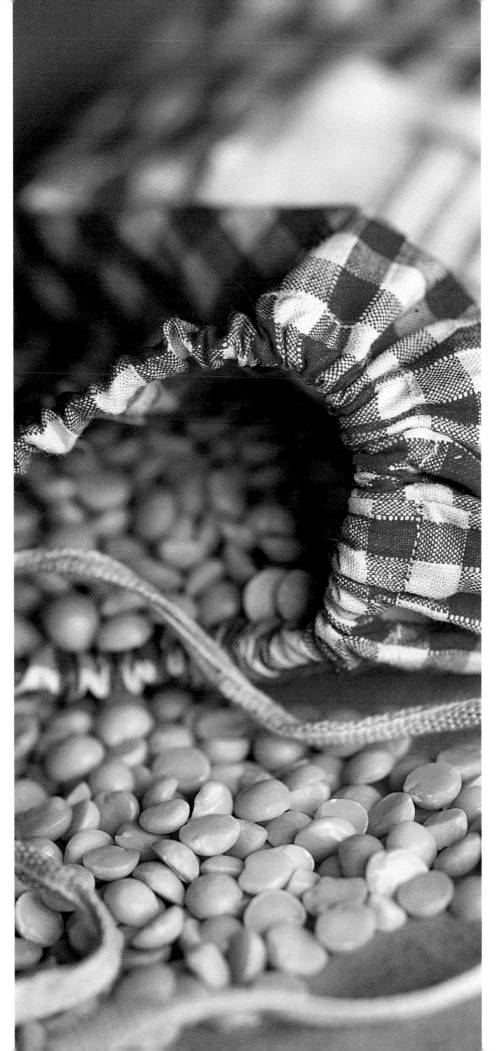

LEFT

*These storage bags are
great for keeping rice
and lentils neat and
tidy. They can be hung
from hooks if you are
short of shelf space.*

ABOVE

This roller towel was made from a vintage linen lined with a light white terrycloth. These bold 1950s floral prints can look great when used sparingly against a stark white background in a contemporary setting.

were well built. Overhead units can be rather oppressive so I replaced them with open shelves right up to the ceiling. These are excellent for storage jars and a place to hook up numerous cups and mugs. I keep half a dozen of our everyday glasses and plates on the shelves just above the dishwasher, which is so much easier than having to put them away on a daily basis. The lower units originally had rather fussy doors but now they have been re-faced with simple panels painted with a fresh white gloss. I was lucky enough to inherit an old flagstone floor, which scrubbed up very well, so the basis of the room is really very simple.

The focal point

The main focus of the room is a big kitchen table. A set of new kitchen chairs are grouped around the pine table, and I have painted them in a strong red paint to match the kitchenware. I had a really pretty set of old kitchen chairs but they were very fragile and were always having to be repaired. The advantage of the new chairs is they are robust enough to take the wear and tear of kitchen life. They are extremely comfortable and the squab seats are easy to take off and wash. If I get bored with the red paint, it would be easy to alter them to a different color. I have covered the seat cushions in a red and white

the kitchen

RIGHT

*This strawberry print
adds a splash of color
in my all-white kitchen.*

OPPOSITE

*These favorite cook
books are covered in
oilcloth or wallpaper
to protect them from
greasy fingers!*

checked cotton on one side and a vintage
print on the other so they can be swapped
around if I feel like a change.

I am still looking for a large enough table for
the room. To improvize, a large piece of wood
from a timber merchant is laid over the
existing table, which is much too small. I did
this as an emergency over Christmas when we
had a full house and it may stay like this for
years. With a tablecloth thrown over the top
no one need ever be any the wiser. Changing
the cloths really alters the feel of a room and
I have collected all sorts over the years.

Fabrics add color

Vintage fabrics can make great tablecloths
and if there are no other patterns in a room,
big bold floral prints can look great on a
table. It is possible to find them already made
into curtains and so long as they are
washable cotton and not interlined they are
easy to convert. They are often the right size
for a 6 foot table and it is usually a case of
just unpicking the heading tape and
hemming along one end. Tablecloths that are
too small can be bordered in either gingham
or plain white linen to fit.

We have a table in the hall, which can be
used for a dining room, but we tend to eat in
the kitchen when we entertain. It is only once
in a while for some special reason that we set

the kitchen

RIGHT

*This vintage floral
tablecloth has been
extended with a wide
white linen border.
The edges are then
finished off in
a contrasting bias
binding.*

OPPOSITE

*Herbs and dried beans
sit in bags in my store
cupboard. They are
made from various
leftover scraps of
tickings and ginghams
and then labeled with
a marker pen.*

OVERLEAF

*Variations of the same
print are used to cover
these painted antique
Swedish chairs.*

up the hall for eating. Instead, if I need to make the kitchen look a bit smarter in the evening, I use a white tablecloth. Vintage French linen sheets are wonderful for this purpose as they have such a rustic quality. They also dye beautifully in the washing machine to make colored cloths. They are quite readily available in antique stores and markets and are very good value compared to traditional damask cloths.

In addition to tablecloths and napkins, tea towels bring color and interest to a kitchen. As mine live on the stove they are always on full display, so I try to have cloths that look cheerful in the room. I love the old floral towels from the 1950s, which are quite hard to find and sometimes have frayed edges. This can be remedied by trimming off the ends and adding a border such as a strip of crocheted lace. It is easy to make your own by simply hemming rectangles of printed linen. Edging the cloths with bias binding, as with the napkins, also looks good.

One of my favorite things in the kitchen is an old floral roller towel. We have a pantry and store room off the kitchen which has a small sink. The roller towel is made from a bright piece of floral linen and hangs on the wall by the sink. The room itself is very stark and practical, whitewashed from top to toe including the concrete floor, with plain larder shelves and storage cupboards. The roller towel is the only print in the room and looks great against such a severe backdrop. I made it from a vintage linen curtain and then lined it with white terrycloth. There is also an old scrubbed pine kitchen table in the room used for chopping vegetables. The original turquoise blue paint remains on the legs, adding some more color to the room.

Storage spaces

In the pantry I store all sorts of food in a glass-fronted cupboard. I was once given some herbs in a striped ticking bag, which gave me the idea of storing other food in bags. This is an excellent way to keep beans and rice and bags are just as easy to use as storage jars. Label them by writing directly on to the bags or a sticky tape with a laundry marker pen. I used up all the pieces of blue, red and white stripes and checks that I had and they do look really pretty all together behind the glass.

The pantry is also the place for keeping shopping bags and baskets. I keep my bread hanging up in a bag as the long loaves never seem to fit in the bread bin and the baskets are excellent for storing fruit and vegetables on the floor. I have made all sorts of bags in a traditional tote shape out of printed upholstery fabrics and have even made some

An overall view of my
kitchen showing some
of my red and white
kitchenware.
The tablecloth is an old
curtain that has been
converted.

from old plaid wool blankets. They are all
lined with canvas as they need to be strong
if they are to be used to carry the shopping.
They are much more practical than using
plastic bags, which always seem to burst,
and they can easily be washed now and then.
I must have at least half a dozen and find
they also come in handy as over-night bags.
I have also lined some large wicker baskets
to use as shopping bags.

Hanging from a hook behind the pantry door
is my carrier bag store. It is a tube of fabric
with an elastic neck at the top and the
bottom. You simply push the plastic bags into
the top and then pull them out one by one
from the bottom. They sell them in our
village at local rummage sales, which is
where I copied the idea. I used to have a
drawer in the kitchen that was bursting with
bags and would never shut so I think they are
the most brilliant idea. They also, with the
right instructions, make excellent presents.
The other obvious present from the kitchen
is home-made jam and marmalade. I am
hopeless at making it so I cheat and buy it
from the local market. It is easy to transform

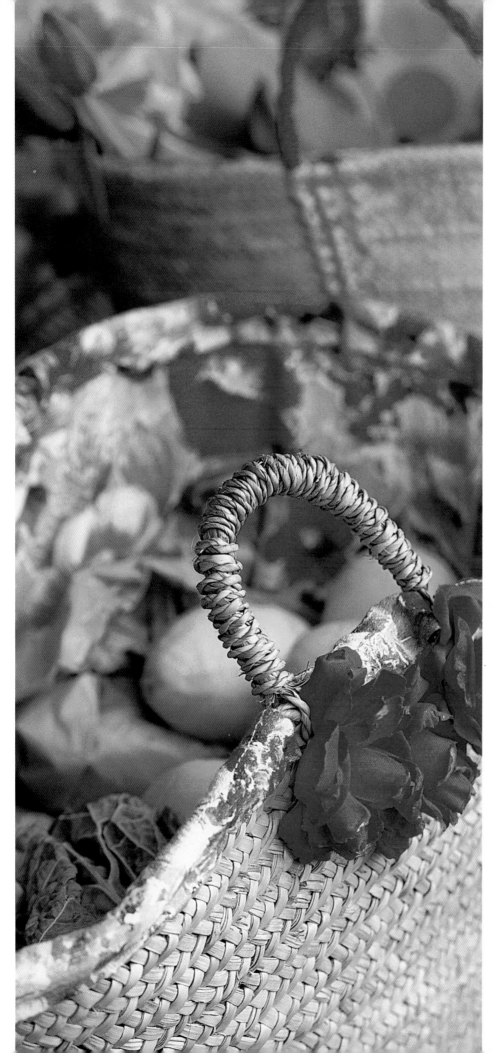

LEFT

This wicker basket had the roses attached when I bought it, but I added the floral lining to make it stronger.

OPPOSITE

Jam pots line up with their floral hats along the pantry shelf.

the jars into gifts by making pretty fabric lids
with a pair of pinking scissors. Rather than
using string or an elastic band, bright-colored
hair elastics are great for attaching the fabric,
and luggage labels are excellent
for the gift tags. It is also easy to decant other
foodstuffs such as biscuits or sweets into
large glass jars and finish them in this way
as presents.

Finishing touches

The other items I have collected in the
kitchen are a wide variety of aprons. You can
still find incredible old aprons in thrift shops
and they come in the most wonderful prints.
My favorite one has different recipes for
cocktails printed all over it and I once had a
great one spelling out the calories of every
conceivable food. They are often very kitsch
but are good fun and amusing to collect.
I also enjoy buying old cookbooks. Besides
the recipes, they often have great illustrations
and very funny pictures of the strangest
combinations of food – roast chicken
decorated with glacé cherries or a 'log' of
gammon and pineapple, for example!
Cookbooks that are used regularly work well
if they are covered in oilcloth or paper jackets
as they can so easily be ruined.
Aside from cooking I really enjoy spending
time in my kitchen. We no longer have a sofa

OPPOSITE

*This tablecloth with its
'sail boat' print has a
rather Dutch feel that
mirrors the painting
behind. I have added a
wide gingham border
to the fabric.*

RIGHT

The trunk of my car –
full of groceries. The
shopping bags are
made from a mixture
of blankets and
printed linen. The
plastic one was a find
from Morocco.

and television in the room so now use our living room on a daily basis. But the stove gives the room a friendly feel and we still all congregate around the kitchen table. If I ever get bored of the blue, red and white color scheme, it would be easy and inexpensive to change. The only item in the room that I would need to keep is the blue stove as the rest cost very little.

I enjoy collecting all the old kitchen ware. There is nothing better than coming across a new item I haven't got – last week I found a red egg timer. The one rule I have when buying something is that it has to be practical. My collection is nearly at saturation point and I am tempted to sell all the red and start again. Perhaps I could go for green next time to mix with the blue. All I would have to do is paint the chairs again, find a few new tablecloths and tea towels, and I would have a brand new room! The possibilities are endless.

Extending the kitchen

Our hall is a fairly empty room with a large fireplace, stone-flagged floor and lots of book shelves. There are two wing chairs by the fire and a round table piled with books in the middle of the room. There is also an old refectory table, which sits against one wall with a couple of lamps on it and usually a big bowl of flowers.

I can use the refectory table as a sideboard and have a large circular table top that fits on to the round table to extend it. I cover the table with a giant felt tablecloth and then put a white cloth on top of this. I use a complete mixture of pairs of chairs from around the house. When I bother to make the effort it is wonderful to eat with the fire blazing on a cold winter's night. I have no wish to have a formal dining room as they always seem such cold rooms, only used for best occasions and rather out of date. Given the choice, I would rather combine a room such as a library with a dining room.

To tie in with all my different tablecloths I use lots of leftover fabric scraps, including tablecloth remnants, for napkins. I tend never to have the right amount in one design, so now have assorted piles – ready-made red checked napkins are mixed with ticking stripes and ginghams. For some strange reason I always end up with five rather than six of a set, just as one sock always disappears in the wash. It doesn't matter if you have only enough fabric for the odd napkin as this can be used to line, say, a bread basket. Bias bindings also make lovely edgings on napkins and tablecloths. This cotton tape is available in the most incredible colors and looks great when the different binding colors are allowed to clash.

the kitchen

Storage bags

I made these bags from scraps of gingham or ticking, but you could just as easily use ready-made shoe bags. Each is made from a length of fabric sewn together up the sides. The top is then stitched down to make a channel into which lengths of cord are fed. I have stuck on linen tape for the labels and written on them with a marker pen. They are easy to pull off when you need to re-label the bags.

Collecting kitchenware

I started off by collecting red and white storage jars but now even have matching pots and pans. It is not always the patterns that match; often it is purely the colors. My one criterion for when I buy something for the kitchen is will I use it? I am just as likely to find something modern in the a retail shop such as my striped mugs as I am a vintage jug in a junk shop.

Food covers

A friend made me this food cover out of
a piece of old 1950s kitchen fabric.
I particularly love the way that she has used
up an old broken necklace to weight the
edges. The beads look positively jewel-like
as well as being so practical. The rickrack
braid is also an easy way to finish off a small
circular hem as you don't have to turn over
the fabric, which can be tricky.

Napkins

Over the years, I have made up numerous
scraps of fabric into napkins and like to use
a combination of materials at any one
time. I tend to collect various red and white
tickings and checks but also have been
known to use the odd piece of floral or
pictorial fabric to add a touch of variety.
I also like to edge ready-made napkins
in contrasting bias bindings for a change.

the laundry

the laundry

I have always considered it the height of luxury to have enough space in a house to have a laundry room. For a long time I lived in a small apartment where the ironing board doubled up as a desk top and I was forever having to hide piles of washing and ironing when friends visited. I dreamt of having a large airing cupboard with space for endless starched white sheets and lavender bags and of being able to hang an old-fashioned drying rack from the ceiling.

Then, quite recently, we moved and at last I had inherited such a room. All too quickly, however, it was commandeered by my husband for his tool kit and vast range of car cleaning products. The only answer has been to build a large cupboard at the back of the room to hide all his clutter along with the vacuum and mops. The rest of the laundry can now remain as clutter-free as possible.

Practicalities

Above all else, a laundry room has to be practical. Besides regular washing and ironing activities, such a room can be used for anything from boot cleaning to dog grooming. The entrance to my laundry is just by the back door and all the muddy boots seem to end up by the sink, so I have laid a blue linoleum floor, which is easy to keep clean. The walls and ceiling are painted with a shiny gloss white paint to withstand all the wear and tear and there is a high shelf around the room where numerous flower vases and pots are stored out of the way. Below it is a peg rail for hanging the ironed laundry.

The sink is under the window so I have made the curtains out of an old pair of striped beach towels – it doesn't matter if they get wet. They have been left unlined and just have ties at the top as opposed to curtain headings so they can be taken down and thrown in the wash. Bath or beach towels can also be a great find to convert into very practical and pretty bathroom curtains.

The laundry cupboard

At the back of the room is a large walk-in cupboard. I had a roll of floral paper left over from my last house which was just enough to paper the walls inside the cupboard. I love the cheerfulness of the very colorful print in an otherwise functional space and the contrast with the rather austere white walls of the rest of the laundry room. There are shelves from floor to ceiling on one side and another peg rail. Shelves like this are the perfect space for storing everything, from the car-cleaning kit to the tool box.

I used to keep all my sewing things in an old trunk and was forever rummaging to find what was needed. There are now so many

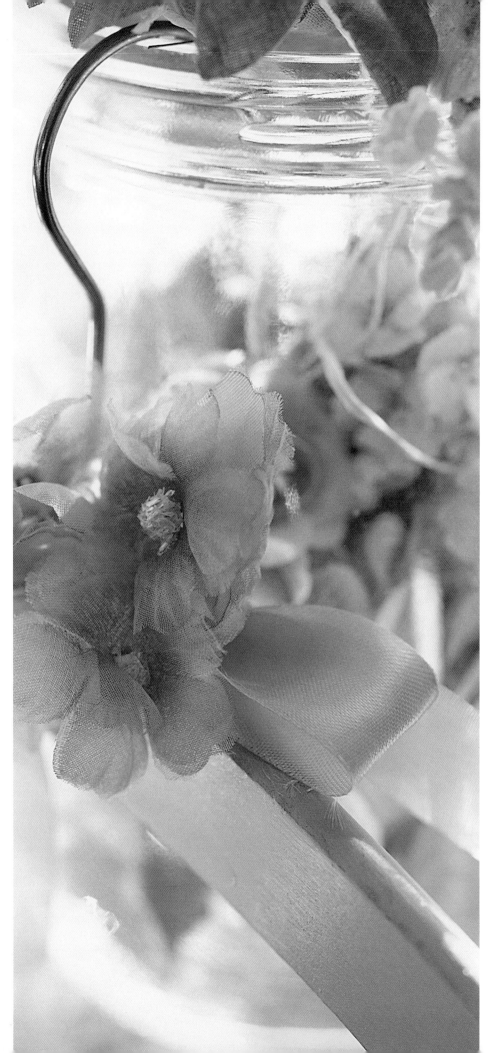

These haberdashery
flowers are great for
decorating all sorts of
things, ranging from
coat hangers to
lavender bags. I keep
my collection stored
away in old glass jars.

43

ribbons and trimmings collected over the years, I can't bear to throw any away. Now, however, they are neatly sorted into a collection of old biscuit tins and glass jars and kept on a shelf in this cupboard, which is so much more practical.

Old wicker baskets are perfect for storing other items such as cleaning products, and a collection of old enamelware buckets really is great for all those messier items such as the shoe-polish kit. The peg rail at the back has become home to part of my endless collection of shopping bags.

The airing cupboard

My actual airing cupboard has been built around the boiler. Because of the heat it generates, the panels on the doors are open so that the air can ventilate. To disguise the doors, I have covered them with lengths of antique toile fabric fitted on to stretchy wire at the top and bottom so it is easy to take them down and wash. The inside of the cupboard has then been finished with simple slatted shelves.

As well as storing sheets and towels and airing washing and ironing, the cupboard acts as a storage place for my large collection of antique quilts and blankets that have been gleaned over the years. Lavender bags and bars of scented soap tucked in between the

OPPOSITE

These lavender bags are very quick to make. Squares of fabric are hand-stitched together and tied like a parcel with a pretty ribbon.

the laundry

blankets keep the moths away – they not only give off a wonderful smell to the room as a whole, but are a great alternative to the rather musty smell of mothballs.

Ways with fabric

I use up all sorts of scraps and ribbons to make lavender bags. I even cut up old clothes such as shirts and nightdresses. I love hand sewing while watching television and find it very therapeutic to run up square parcels to fill with lavender. Each one is then finished off with a ribbon tie. It is possible to make

piles of them in an evening and they make great gifts as well as being useful at home. I have got rather in the habit of making them in squares but have in the past made all sorts of different shapes and sizes – rectangles and circles, both large and small, are just as straightforward.

I have also begun to make a wide collection of decorative coat hangers. I found some wonderful knitted hangers in a local antique store and then began to play around with the idea of making my own. I started with a scrap of leftover fabric from the laundry cupboard

These knitted coat hangers are a favorite of mine bought in my local market. I love the random choice of colors that are used in the stripes.

47

the laundry

My ironing board has a cover made from an old floral fabric. It is lined with a heat-resistant fabric and finally fitted with a draw string.

This clothespin bag hangs from a coat hanger on the washing line. The fabric is edged in bright pink bias binding.

the laundry

curtains, covering one and adding some old hat flowers. I also covered some hangers in a selection of brightly colored silk lining fabric and trimmed them with some tiny fabric roses from a department store. As well as using them in the laundry room I leave hangers covered in this way hanging out in a row on the peg rails in the guest rooms instead of having a wardrobe, as it leaves much more space.

Washing and ironing

One of my favorite things about living in the country is being able to dry my washing out in the fresh air on warm and – preferably – windy days. There is nothing better than the smell of freshly aired clothes. I now have a hugely long clothesline strung up in our orchard.

One of the essential items for a clothesline is a clothespin bag and I made mine from a piece of printed dress fabric. Cut out two pieces of fabric the same shape. Trace the outline of a wooden coat hanger for the top and then make the bag so that it is narrower in the middle so the clothespins don't fall out in the wind. Leave an opening on one side and edge this with some bias binding for a neat and colorful finish. A bag like this is easy to make and could also be used as a good general storage bag.

OPPOSITE

I used a leftover roll of
wallpaper to brighten
up my cleaning
cupboard. I love the
way this rather smart
paper looks so out
of context with the
assorted contents.

LEFT

This favorite cup has
been chipped so I use
it to measure my soap
powder rather than
throw it out.

the laundry

RIGHT

This coat hanger was covered with a leftover scrap from the airing cupboard curtains and then trimmed with some vintage hat flowers.

OPPOSITE

My airing cupboard showing my sheets and blankets on a very tidy day!

When I had my small apartment, the ironing board was always on show in the kitchen. I was horrified by the choice of covers available in the shops so I converted a wonderful old floral curtain into a cover and it became part of the decoration.

Ironing board covers are easy to make (see page 54) but it is important to be sure you use a flameproof lining. Trace the pattern from the old ironing board cover and finish it with a draw string so that it's easy to take off and wash each time you feel the need. Each time a cover wears out, it is simple to add a

new one on top – the board gets more and more padded, too, which is particularly great for the ironing!

Now that I have a proper space for my laundry I am quite happy to spend hours in the wash room. In the winter, I find that it is the coziest place in the house. There is nothing like the smell of lavender and clean washing mixed with the reassuring sound of the boiler starting up throughout the day. If only I had just that little bit of extra space I would install an armchair and even a television and really settle in.

the laundry

Ironing board cover

This ironing board cover is made from a piece of old cotton curtain fabric. It is lined with a heavy-duty flameproof curtain interlining and fitted with a draw string so it is easy to take off and wash. Use heavyweight cotton as this lasts longer and be sure that the fabric does not have any man-made content, which could be flammable. These covers are the top-selling item in my shop.

Useful ribbon ties

It is very practical to keep pairs of sheets tied together in my linen cupboard. It can be hard to tell which size sheets are once they are put away, so to save the bother of opening them up to find out, I use different-colored ribbons to represent single or double when putting them away. Here I have used pale green and lilac ribbons and as long as they are loosely tied, the ribbons can be recycled.

Decorative coat hangers

These decorative coat hangers make
wonderful gifts and are simple to make. It's
easiest to cover a coat hanger that is already
padded. I pin the fabric so that its seam runs
across the top, which can then be hand
stitched. I have collected a wide range of
haberdashery flowers to use as decoration.
I tie the stalks to the base of the coat hanger
and then tie a piece of ribbon over the top.

Lavender parcels

These lavender parcels are an excellent way
of using up old scraps. I tend to use fabrics
with mini-print designs in pastel colors and
finish them off with scraps of clashing
ribbons for the ties. It is worth buying the
best quality filling as it lasts so much longer.
Cheap lavender has often not been properly
dried and has a tendency to go off and
smell vile in no time.

the living room

the living room

RIGHT

These children's chairs fit well beside a fireplace and can come in handy as extra seating. The pile of books was a simple way to add to the pink theme of the room.

My priority in decorating a living room is that it should be comfortable and have a friendly feel to it. Many homes these days have a cozy study or family room that is used on a regular basis with the best room in the house left as the more formal living room. This only gets opened up for entertaining and as a result rarely looks lived in or has the charm of the other room. While I have two separate living rooms at home I have tried to use them both as much as possible. Inevitably, the room with the television wins over, but seriously comfortable armchairs and a big log fire do help to entice people next door.

Starting points

I am fortunate to have a fireplace in each room. I find it hard to decorate a living room without one and in the past have made a false chimney breast where one was missing in order to center the room. I set about decorating the television room around the colors of a rather unusual old Turkish rug, in very strong reds and turquoises with yellow accents, which is large enough to fill most of the room. The walls were painted white and they remain so as I am still deciding whether to leave them or go for a color. Some fairly bright contemporary paintings are the main feature in the room and they look good set against the plain whitewash for now.

The curtains are made out of inexpensive coarse yellow linen and they are edged with scarlet velvet – I like these two textures together. The curtains are a very simple shape, made with gathered headings on an antique curtain pole.

There is also a small side door into the garden from this room. It has a light printed curtain hung across it for when the room becomes too bright when the door is open in the summer.

Chair covers

Frequently the main choice that has to be made in a living room is how to cover the upholstered furniture. I already had two sofas and a couple of armchairs to use in the room. I have either inherited or bought them in antique stores and so they are all old. With a few exceptions, I much prefer to use old furniture as it is often beautifully made and has much more character than brand new pieces. Also it is often very much cheaper. I chose the pieces to use in this room strictly by their comfort factor.

The two sofas needed reupholstering rather than loose covering, so I chose the same yellow linen as the curtains for one and a faded red to go with the rug for the other. Because children and dogs use the room constantly and muddy paws often leave a

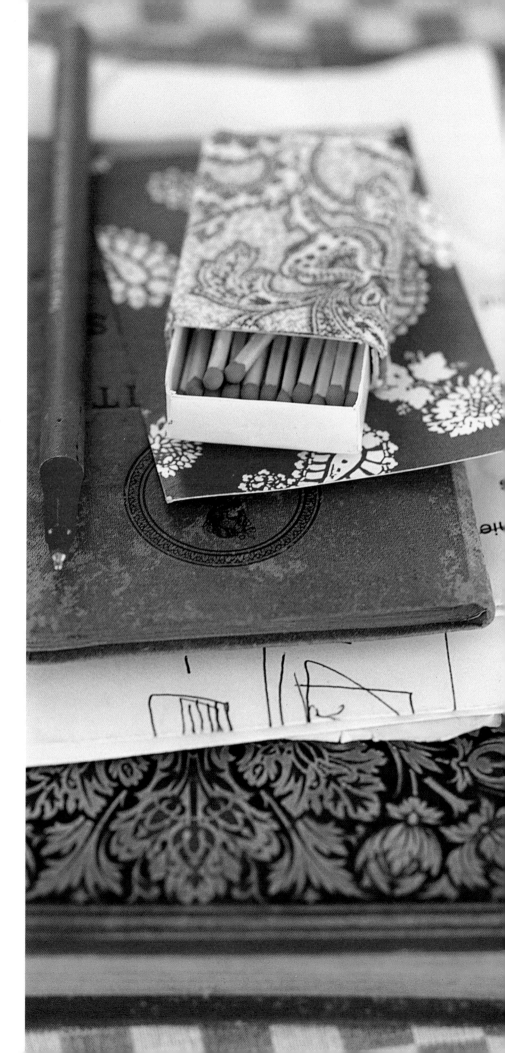

the living room

RIGHT

The pink and white coloring of the room even extends to a scrap of fabric on a matchbox.

OPPOSITE

An antique tablecloth is reflected in the mirror of this urban living room. The simple color scheme helps to give the room a calm ambience.

the living room

trail over the furniture, I decided to cover the seat cushions with old fabric. I found a bright yellow velvet curtain at a jumble sale to tuck over the yellow sofa and have an antique paisley quilt strewn over the red one. These stronger colors would be too much for a whole cover but are great just for the seats. They are also easy to take off and clean and then throw back on again.

The armchairs were already covered in faded linens and although not ideal, work perfectly well for the time being with the decoration in the rest of the room. I have yet to decide what to cover them in, so to bring them in with the rest of the room, brightly colored rugs are folded over the backs to add some color. I have a feeling they may stay like this for some time!

Finally, there was one wing chair left and it needed a loose cover to disguise its rather sickly velvet upholstery. Some pink and red ticking went well, but there wasn't nearly enough. The answer was to patch the back with another fabric. Rather than try to match it, I used a clashing piece of Moroccan striped awning cotton.

Colorful pillows

The pillows are the main other decoration in the room. Old shawls make excellent covers – for this room I used some in red and

LEFT

The colors of this little painting on the mantelpiece are reflected in the living room itself.

OPPOSITE

Flowers make a huge difference in this living room. They add to the color and prevent it from feeling too stark.

63

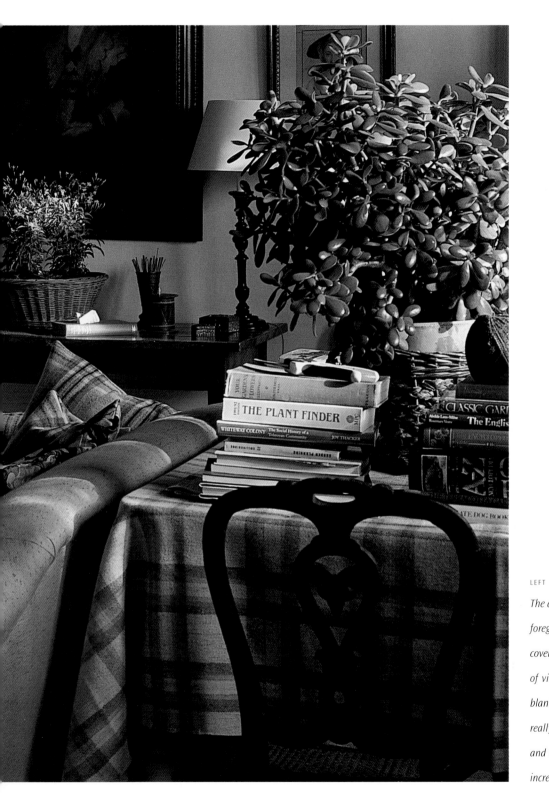

The armchair in the
foreground has been
covered in a patchwork
of vintage Welsh
blankets. These are
really hard-wearing
and woven in the most
incredible colors.

the living room

turquoise stripes, putting clashing fringes around the edge. An old red paisley shawl has also been cut up to mix with these. I had planned to have nothing floral but I relented when I came across two old sample pieces of fabric with a huge bunch of flowers on each piece. The colors were an uncanny match to the rest of the room. They are now made up with pink ticking borders similar to the fabric on the wing chair and sit in the center of each sofa.

Bits and bobs

The rest of the room is fairly simple. A blue-painted washstand, which introduces more color, is used as a side table, and one of my favorite things is a toy box of a similar blue that has a wooden cut-out frieze of dogs similar to my own terrier Stanley. I have converted it into a log box and it sits under another side table.

I tried to entice Stanley off the sofa – to no avail – by giving him a wonderful patchwork knitted blanket in his basket. I love these colorful throws and have recently started to collect them. The best place to find them is in junk stores and garage sales.

The television takes up most of another table, again covered in a paisley quilt. It seemed pointless to make any attempt to hide it as it is the center of attention in the room. Apart

A view across my television room in the country. I have recently begun collecting the patchwork wool blankets as seen in the foreground.

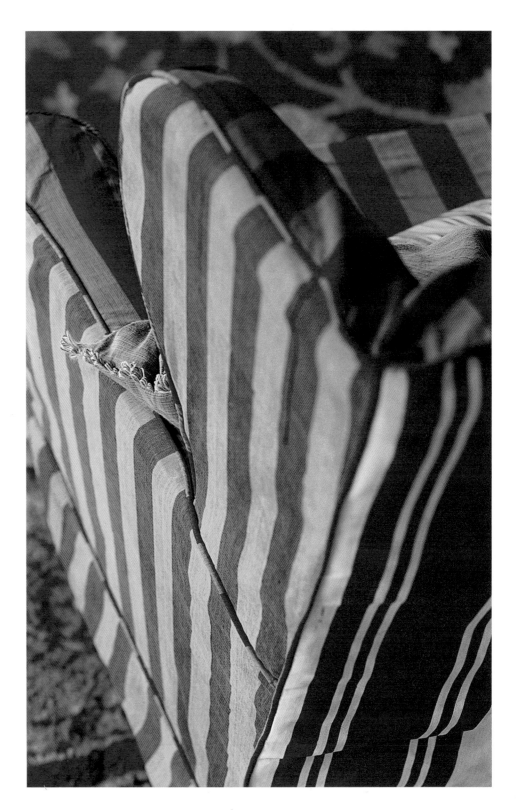

The back of this chair has been covered with a contrasting ticking as I didn't have quite enough fabric for the whole chair.

from a low, white-painted table, which is useful in front of the sofa, the rest of the furniture is made up of old wooden pieces, including a book shelf and simple side tables, that I have acquired from various sources. In the summer, when the door is open into the garden and the sun streams in, this room really is a riot of color.

A more neutral setting

The living room next door has a wonderful big fireplace and flagstone floor. This has a much more wintry feel with lots of book shelves and darker furniture. Again, the room is whitewashed and here I shall definitely keep it that way. There is an old Dutch oil painting that hangs with early needlework pictures and some engravings that suit the simplicity of the plain walls. The window has such a pretty stone surround I am loathe to hang any curtains. The fireplace really is the best thing in here and we do spend plenty of time, particularly in the winter, sitting around a roaring fire.

The wall-to-wall book shelves form the major decoration in the room and even more books are piled high on a table behind the sofa. As time goes by I am quite sure that they will spill on to neighboring chairs, but I don't think you can ever have too many books in a room. (I often choose paint colors from the colors of cloth books. They come in the most fantastic shades and it is much easier to take a book to the paint store and have the color matched than it is to choose your preferred shade from a tiny swatch.)

Welsh blankets

The armchair that I wanted to use in this room has been covered in a patchwork of the darker shades of Welsh blankets. The leftover pieces have been used for some pillows. I made these by combining the plaids with some old black chintz, so they can be used either way round on the sofa. I also mixed the chintz with some old red ticking to add to the variety. The black floral fabric mixed with the plaids helps to prevent the room from being too serious.

Something a little airier

My living room in London is quite different again. It is a light space with a more modern feel. It is painted white, but here the floor is left with simple bleached floorboards and no rugs. The color scheme, inspired by an old tablecloth, is simply pink, black and white. Once the colors had been decided on I was able to look out for things especially for the room – two pink children's chairs caught my eye in a junk shop and also a tiny scrap of pink and white toile came in handy to cover

the living room

Extra seating

I use these kids chairs as side tables in the
living room but as long as they are armless
they can also come in handy for extra seating.
They are easy to tuck away by the side of a
fireplace and bring out in an emergency.
Being old school chairs, they are easy to find
in natural wood, but are quickly and readily
transformed to whatever color you choose
with a plain coat of paint.

Clashing colors

I added this shocking pink bias binding to
this striped pillow to cheer it up. The bow
also acts as a practical closure. If I cannot find
an exact match to something, I prefer to use
a completely clashing color instead.
Trimmings and bindings are an especially
easy way to do this. Bias bindings are great
value for this purpose and are available in
a huge range of colors and widths.

Patchwork blankets

I have recently started to collect these
fantastically colorful patchwork blankets.
They are easiest to find in charity shops
or flea markets and come in all shapes and
sizes. The best ones have crocheted edges and
wicked color combinations. Besides using
them as the more conventional blanket
or throw they also convert into excellent
pillow covers or dog rugs.

Flowers

I could happily spend a fortune each week
buying flowers for the house but quite often
get away with buying just the cheapest of
the bunch. I try to mix together a few
clashing colors – say three shades of pink
or a jumble of orange and pink – and simply
pile them into a jug or vase. I do think they
make the whole difference to making a house
feel alive and lived in.

the bedroom

the bedroom

From a decorating point of view, the bedroom is my favorite room in the house. I have a passion for floral fabrics and old-fashioned rosy prints in particular and left to my own devices could happily use them throughout the house. The bedrooms are the one area where I feel I can really use these prints. I find there is a big difference between having a room that is pretty and fresh and somewhere that is too frilly and overly feminine and it is always a case of trying to strike a good balance.

My bedroom

My own bedroom is lilac, green and white. This color scheme stemmed from an oil painting of mauve hydrangeas left to me by my aunt which I like very much. I also had a set of French engravings with old-fashioned green mounts. With these in mind I set out to look for material for the curtains. I already had a wonderful scrap of chintz printed with violets that was ideal, but there was only enough to make a couple of pillows. I searched everywhere for a new material to use but to no avail. So in the end, I had a fabric printed in the colorway of my own choosing. There are a few companies that will print their own designs to any color for not much more cost than usual. This particular material now features large in the bedroom,

appearing as curtains and on the bed head and valance.

I then painted the walls pale green, only to find the room looked rather gloomy. There can be a tendency with some old-fashioned floral fabrics for the room to end up looking like it belongs to a very old lady! In my case, I found that an old purple quilt helped to cheer it up but the walls needed changing. The end result is white panels over the green, leaving the color in wide borders around the edges of the room. A purple wash line has been painted on the edge of the green bands. I am so pleased with how the white has lifted the room and with the way the panelling has worked that I have reproduced it in another room in a different color.

Bed dressing

My favorite thing in the room is a giant patchwork blanket that I have made. Although it was easy to do, it took ages as I am really slow at knitting. I chose four colors for the wool to form a checkered pattern on the blanket and made each square about 6 inches wide. Once the squares were knitted, they were quick to sew together and the sense of satisfaction once it was finished was immense.

I have an aversion to quilts and like nothing better than linen sheets and old-fashioned

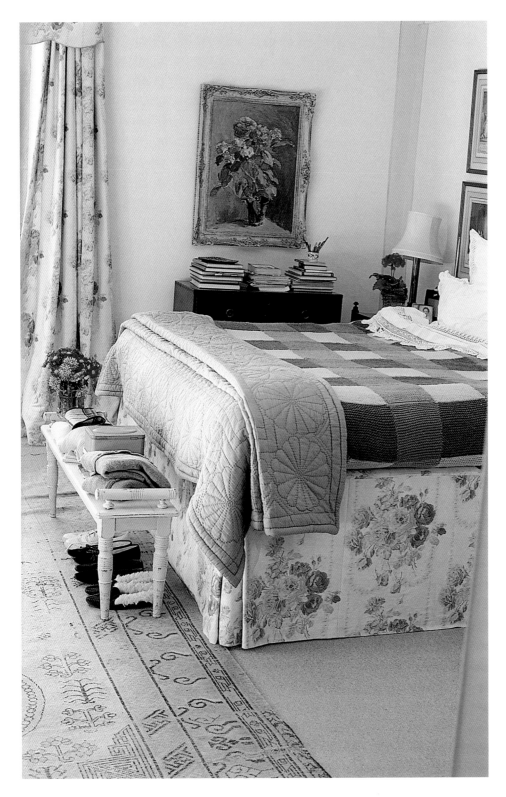

*The color scheme
for this bedroom
originated from the
oil painting of mauve
hydrangeas hanging
on the far wall. The
fabric on the bed
valance and curtains
was specially colored
by a fabric
manufacturer to
match an old pillow.*

the bedroom

*A colorful silk lining
and pale blue bobble
fringe updates this
vintage violet chintz.*

*My knitted blanket in
progress!*

the bedroom

blankets. I prefer to use plain white linen in this room and have collected quite a lot over the years. It is easy to find pretty antique pillowcases decorated with lace but double sheets are more difficult. Plain sheets can, however, be transformed by sewing heavy cotton lace on to their edges.

Small details

The rest of the room is furnished quite simply. An antique mahogany chest of drawers and a laundry press prevent it from being too feminine, and an armchair is newly covered in a simple fresh green and white striped ticking.

The window seat is the only other area where there is more floral fabric. I have made up the pillows from the original piece of violet fabric and introduced some pale blue into the lilac and green color scheme in the way of a couple of pillows and bobble fringe. It helps to inject some extra color into a room, as if everything matches too closely it can look rather contrived. This said, I was delighted to be given my purple fluffy slippers and old-fashioned green radio to go in the room.

The rose room

For the spare bedroom I already had a bed covered in pink roses and some curtains to

RIGHT

A selection of my old feather eiderdowns. They can still be found in perfect condition with these pretty paisley covers.

OPPOSITE

A cozy pink hot-water bottle cover has been enlivened with scraps of lime green ribbon.

The delicate organza

lampshade standing

beside the bed was

made by stitching the

fabric carefully on to

an old wire frame.

match left from my previous apartment. I love this material so was happy to decorate the room around it. The walls are painted a faded turquoise blue, a color that I like very much with pink. I then framed a number of favorite Redouté rose prints in simple white frames to hang in sets on the walls to break up the expanse of blue.

Because this is a guest room I have fixed up a peg rail for hanging any clothes on rather than installing a wardrobe. It leaves so much more space in the room. Some pretty covered coat hangers are on the rail to add to the decoration.

Old-fashioned bedding

Old-fashioned candy-striped cotton sheets with matching pillowcases are on the bed. These are a favorite of mine and are still made these days in all sorts of colors.

A mixture of comforters and blankets is then piled on top – there is an old-fashioned pale green comforter with a pink lining for the bed cover and a faded pink and green plaid throw for the top blanket.

I love these vintage rugs that come from Wales. They can be found in the prettiest colors and are excellent for upholstery as well as blankets. Several similar but different ones upholster the bedroom chairs. They are applied like patchwork with a different rug

LEFT
A peg rail acts as an alternative to a wardrobe in my spare bedroom.

BELOW
I bought this basket with the pretty lining from an antique shop, but the lining would be easy to make.

the bedroom

with a small silk taffeta frill and ties. Some dry-cleaners will still re-cover eiderdowns in your own fabric, which is useful.

Adding a touch of freshness

In another spare bedroom, I have used some old paisley material that is similar to the eiderdowns. This room has an old four-poster bed with rose chintz curtains that I am fond of as it is something I grew up with. The lining of the curtains was a rather dull beige print, but now it is a simple yellow striped cotton, which I find most cheerful. I have used the same stripe at the windows, edged with a pink bias binding.

By painting the room pure white – including the beams – and using white-painted furniture next to the mahogany bed, the space has been kept as fresh and light as possible.

Again, I have used heavy, lace-edged sheets and pillowcases on the bed with a pale Welsh blanket and an eiderdown on top. There are all sorts of pillowcases that I can use in this room. For example, I found some pretty dress-making fabrics in linen and brushed cotton that have made up well into covers. They look really pretty edged with haberdashery lace and are very easy to make. I mix them up with plain white or colored linen sheets.

LEFT

The window seat in my bedroom has pillows made from my favorite violet fabric. They are lined in lime green silk and trimmed with ice-blue bobble fringe to add some extra color.

87

the bedroom

A small touch

I found it hard to find a good lampshade for beside the bed in this room so I re-covered an existing shade in striped organza. I gathered the fabric around the top of the frame and once this was stitched into place it was easy to attach to the bottom of the frame in the same way. To cover the stitching, I finished off the lampshade by sewing on a frill over both top and bottom.

Shapes of old lampshades often have far more character than the ones available now and it is easy to find them in junk shops. Even if they are covered in some hideous fabric, you can have them professionally re-covered in your own favorites.

Stylish variety

I have had such fun decorating these bedrooms. Although the formula for each room is similar, I have tried to give each one a completely different character. But above all, I hope the spare rooms are comfortable and hospitable for my guests. The beds are definitely warm and cozy with their blankets and eiderdowns and I make sure there is always a hot-water bottle ready on cool evenings and cookies by the bed along with the clean linen sheets. I have one more room to do and maybe this time I shall decorate a bedroom without a floral print in sight.

This linen cover was

dyed green in the

washing machine.

The blanket is trimmed

in the same print as

the pillowcase.

A pile of pillowcases

are made from

lightweight linen and

dress-making lace.

This table is an old

friend that I painted

white especially for

the bedroom.

the bedroom

RIGHT

This armchair is covered in vintage blankets, similar to others in the room.

OPPOSITE

The antique fabric on the bed, the prints and the postcards all help to create the 'rose' theme in this spare bedroom.

the bedroom

Color matching

While I have no wish to have a room that is color coordinated from top-to-toe, I was very pleased to find these cozy pajamas that matched my spare bedroom just perfectly. An object like a brightly colored dressing gown hanging on the back of the door forms just as much of the decoration as anything else. It is these small points that can add so much to the finished effect.

Dress fabrics

This blanket had frayed edges so rather than dispose of it altogether, I have trimmed it with some printed cotton to hide the damage. I used the same print to make the pillowcases too, so they make a sort of matching bed set. It is easy to make floral print pillowcases from children's dress fabrics and they are often available in the softest cotton.

Leftover wallpaper

Besides disguising my medical dictionary
with a wallpaper jacket, I have found all sorts
of other ways to use up leftover rolls and
remains of rolls. I have lined my chest of
drawers with different papers and covered
old cardboard boxes for storage. It doesn't
matter if each drawer has a different print,
so even the shortest scrap of leftover paper
can be used.

Blankets

It is easy to buy old wool blankets these days
as so many people choose to use quilts
instead. They are one of the best bargains
in second-hand shops and good quality ones
will usually wash well in the washing
machine. There is nothing better than getting
into a bed made up properly with a cozy
blanket or two and newly laundered sheets
smelling of fresh air.

the bathroom

the bathroom

One of my priorities when house hunting
was to have a bathroom with natural light
and I am fortunate to now have not just one,
but several, large windows in my bathroom.
In fact, the room is one of the largest in the
house, converted from the room the
previous owners used as a master bedroom.
It faces the road and the smaller room at
the back was used as a spare bedroom with
the original bathroom tucked away on a
half-landing.

When we moved in, we felt it made sense to
have the bedroom at the back of the house,
which is much quieter and has a wonderful
view. So now the front bedroom has been
converted into a large bathroom and dressing
room and the half-landing room has become
a small spare bedroom.

Filling the space

As well as a big bath in the middle of the
room there was room for an entire wall of
built-in clothes cupboards to be built. Hidden
among them is a shower. The sink stands at
one end of the room set into an old
cupboard, which doubles up as a dressing
table. Opposite is the original fireplace, which
has been converted to gas. To add to the
feeling of space, two armchairs sit on either
side of the fireplace, one with a terrycloth
loose cover. This is a great place to sit and dry

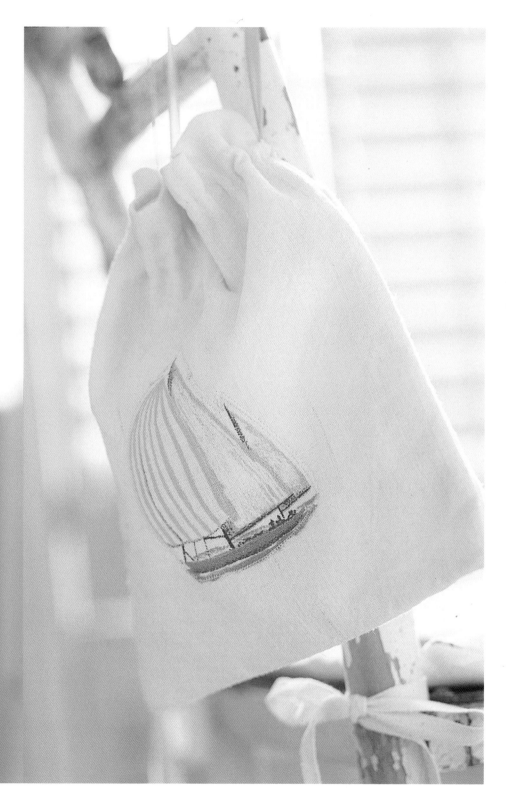

OPPOSITE

*This heavy cotton lace
was simple to add to
the plain white towels
and is strong enough
to withstand plenty
of washing.*

LEFT

*This last scrap of boat
fabric was just enough
for appliquéing on to
a washbag.*

the bathroom

LEFT

I really appreciate the luxury of having a fireplace in my bathroom. The armchair on the left was re-covered in terrycloth especially for the room and is now a great place to sit and dry one's hair.

LEFT

*These wooden shutters
keep out prying eyes
and they allow the
light to stream through
on a sunny day.*

OPPOSITE

*I am very fond of this
picture: a self-portrait
of my favorite great
aunt in the bath!*

one's hair by the fire. There is even room
for a pair of antique wardrobes and another
armchair at the other end of the room.
I could also fit in an old free-standing coat
stand, which I painted white and now use to
hang up the bathrobes and towels.

Creating the atmosphere

The room is painted a cream-colored off-
white and because it faces out on to the street
there are louvered shutters at the windows for
privacy. All the woodwork is painted a pale
shade of 'French' gray. I also have a collection

of Victorian seaside pictures with shell frames
I wanted to use but was concerned that using
shells to decorate the bathroom was a bit of
a cliché. I then came across some 1950s'
scenic boat fabric, which had a quite funky
feel to it. Through combining this with the
seaside pictures, it gave them more character.
As there wasn't much fabric I tried to make
the most of it, using it for pillows and a squab
seat. I had a baby deck chair that I couldn't
resist covering as well to add to the seaside
atmosphere of the room. Now it sits
comfortably by the fireplace. The leftover

the bathroom

pieces I then cut out and used as appliqué on some washbags.

I also had some vintage terrycloth with fishes printed on it which suited the room, so I made this into towels and washcloths by edging it in bias binding. Rather than hang the pictures, they all sit stacked along the mantelpiece, mixed with a collection of colorful plastic mirrors from Morocco and a ship in a bottle. I love this room, particularly when the light is streaming in through the shutters and I can almost feel I am on holiday.

Introducing color

The spare bathroom is painted white, including the floorboards, but it is a much more colorful room than the other one. I found an old piece of floral fabric with bunches of lilac, pink and yellow flowers on a fresh white background that I felt would suit the chairs in this room. It also conveniently matched a bright flower painting that I had, so I set about decorating the room around these colors.

There are some pink fluffy bath mats and all the spare colored towels are stacked together on a green shelf unit which is useful for extra storage. I then found some heavy lace edging to trim the bath towels and some brightly colored braid to decorate the linen hand towels. There are also some hand towels

*This old 'boat' print
pillow cheers up the
kilim chair. Some
of these old pictorial
fabrics have a
wonderful humor
to them.*

*Emery boards sit on
the mantelpiece among
various ships.*

the bathroom

LEFT

The colors for this bathroom were taken from the floral print of the pillow fabric.

RIGHT

These luminous false flowers echo the painting hanging directly behind.

106

the bathroom

made from a floral printed linen, again edged
with heavy cotton lace.

A vase of very false-looking flowers sits on the
top of the shelves in front of the flower
painting, which adds to the color. Flowers can
be fun if they look fake rather than trying to
be real.

Finally, I gathered up a variety of glass jars
and filled them with different-colored bubble
baths and cotton balls to fill the shelves. One
large candy jar is full of various colored
soaps. They come in such pretty pale colors
that look good when they are grouped
together and they also look good when they
are put on a window sill with the light
streaming through. The advantage of
decorating a room like this is that the end
result is bright and airy and it is very simple
to put together.

Past reflections

I once had a very small flat and was able to
make the bathroom out of a tiny room at the
back which had a door opening out on to the
garden. It was wonderful in the summer to
have the door wide open with a great view on
to the garden. Although I had to sacrifice the
space I had used up by having a smaller
kitchen, I felt it was well worth it. I feel very
fortunate to have such a large and airy space
for my present bathroom.

LEFT

My collection of glass bottles is grouped in the bathroom and filled with different colored bubble baths.

OPPOSITE

This floral print hand towel is made from an old furnishing fabric and trimmed with cotton lace.

the bathroom

Hand towels

Old linen hand towels are easy to pick up but are often damaged where there is drawn thread work. This can easily be disguised by stitching a trimming over the top. Here I have used an embroidered edging, but rickrack or lace work just as well. I also like to make hand towels from old floral fabrics – the photograph on the previous page shows just one example, finished with some lace edging.

Washbags

All sorts of material can be used to make washbags so long as they can be washed. Here I used up some scraps of fabric as appliqué, hand stitching them on to a small zip purse. Draw string washbags are the easiest to make (rather like those featured in the kitchen on page 38) and if you choose the right fabric they can look great hanging from a bathroom shelf.

Glass jars

I have quite a mixture of old glass pots and bottles that I like to use in the bathroom. Huge glass candy jars are handy for storing away the bath toys or makeup. A jam pot is perfect to fit cotton swabs and old glass decanters look especially pretty when they are filled with different colored bubble baths. Arranged in rows or groups on a shelf or windowsill they look wonderful.

Toilet paper holders

I think that old waste-paper bins or baskets are just perfect for storing toilet paper in the bathroom. I keep this particular old wire basket in my spare bathroom and ensure that it is piled high at all times with different colored papers. Some people consider colored toilet paper to be the height of bad taste, but I love to see all those pastel colors mixed together!

children's rooms

I have such strong memories of my own bedroom as a child. My first room had pink curtains with a bobble fringe and fluffy white candlewick bed cover. I then progressed to pale blue walls and rosy printed curtains and finally was allowed up to the attic to make my own den. The excitement of being able to choose my own decoration was immense. It was a shrine to the Pony Club, rosettes proudly pinned up alongside pictures of my favorite show jumper. These were gradually replaced with the obligatory posters of pop stars and a lava lamp.

I was terribly envious of my friends who had quilts and modern furniture, as I slept in an old brass bed with an eiderdown. I now really appreciate the fact that my parents let me make my room into my own space from a fairly early age but were also able to guide me with their own taste.

Today's rooms

We have an attic in our house which is totally children's territory. There are two bedrooms and a miniature bathroom. The larger room belongs to my stepdaughter Jessica so has been decorated very much to suit her. It is really tempting for me as a decorator to want to make the room pretty and have it full of the floral fabrics and vintage toys that I love. I had to really edit my taste and try to choose

LEFT

The crocheted pillows on the bed were made from an old blanket. There is a colorful mix of prints in the room.

OVERLEAF

These pictures were made from scraps of old scenic fabrics, which are mainly of views and farmyard scenes. They are simply stapled around boards.

things to suit her rather than myself. I made sure she had the final say in my choice of materials and colors.

Jessica's bedroom

The starting point was when I found a length of old 1950s' kids' fabric, which Jess luckily liked. I used this for the curtains and as the fabric was quite narrow, bordered it with gingham. There was then enough left over to cover a toy box and make some pillows. The room had a lovely old painted door with glass panels, which I kept and simply covered the glass in the same fabric.

The bed sits across the room under the window and is now covered in a mixture of pillows so it can also be used as a sofa. I love brightly colored woolen crochet blankets and have converted some into pillow covers. These are teamed up with old ticking stripes and checks. The bed has side curtains, which can be drawn right across, and they seem to be a never-ending source of entertainment for hide-and-seek. They are made from simple red gingham to match the border of the main curtains.

The desk in the room is an old side table covered in one of my oilcloth fabrics. This material is so practical and cheerful in children's rooms – it makes a perfect work top that is excellent for painting on and all

sorts of other mess. All the furniture in the room is old, picked up in junk shops and then painted in bright colors. I like the fact that nothing is too precious and it doesn't really matter if it gets broken.

The original pink wallpaper is still up and is soon to be changed. Jess has recently become quite a tomboy so it may be a sports-themed paper next, or we might paint an entire wall in blackboard paint, which she can then use as a drawing board. We may do graffiti all over the pink wallpaper before we repaint, which would be fun. There is red linoleum in the bathroom at present and I am considering replacing the bedroom carpet with more linoleum as it works so well.

The room next door

The spare children's bedroom has been painted white with splashes of a big blue floral paper in the window frames and curtains to match. The main decoration is in the old-fashioned children's pictures all over the walls and in the bed linen, which is a mixture of floral printed quilt covers and comforters. There is another table covered in oilcloth, this time stapled over the top, which comes in handy as a changing table when any babies come to stay. There is also an old Moses basket that I had left from home which I had fun re-lining. I bought some

children's rooms

RIGHT

This upholstered child's chair has a matching pillow backed with a bold striped cotton.

OPPOSITE

The toy box was covered in the same vintage children's fabric with a dark blue velvet base to withstand wear and tear. The desk has an oilcloth tablecloth, which is handy for painting and homework.

white flannel for the sheets and trimmed it with the same design as the oilcloth – that of a rosebud print – but in a different colorway. Putting different variations of the same print together can work well, so I made a new slipcover for the comforter in a third color. I have used gingham again in this room. This time it is in the lampshades, to give some sense of continuity.

Making a den

The main play area is away from the house, over in our barn. There is an attic room above the stables which has yet to be restored, and I set it up as a playroom in an emergency one summer holiday. Most of the room was put together in a couple of days and it is so popular we have yet to change it. I love collecting old cowboy fabrics when in America, so this was an obvious place for me to use them.

The room has lovely old beams and rough brick walls, which made it easy to decorate. Some old 'Roy Rogers' woven curtains hang at the window and above the entrance. I also have all sorts of pieces of old scenic fabrics with farmyards and mountain views printed on them. They were perfect to make into pictures. Having measured the sizes of each image, I had some pieces of wooden board cut and then stapled the fabric over the top.

119

LEFT

This playroom has been converted from an attic room in our barn. The wall and floor have been left in their original state.

OVERLEAF LEFT

Vintage 'Roy Rogers' curtains hang at the entrance as part of the cowboy theme.

OVERLEAF RIGHT

It has been fun to accessorize the room with the occasional stetson and cactus.

children's rooms

RIGHT

A bold rose print wallpaper is used around the window recesses. The rest of the room is painted white.

OPPOSITE

An old kitchen table has an oilcloth top so it can be used as a changing table. The spare children's bedroom is decorated with old-fashioned rosebud fabrics and vintage prints.

I have painted bright red. I then added to the color with some bright red blankets. A pretty red and white chest of drawers and some bright Lloyd loom furniture complete the setting. The rest of the furniture is quite rustic – an old garden table that worked as a desk and some garden chairs are dotted about the room for extra seating.

Children seem to love it in the barn. The cowboy decoration is really popular and I am surprised there aren't more contemporary fabrics with this theme. It is fun adding to the room by pinning up the odd old horseshoe or sitting a cactus plant on the window sill. Apart from the fact that it gets quite cold in the winter as there is no insulation yet, I see no need to restore the room. The roughness of the walls and floorboards is part of its charm and the children can be as messy as they like as there is very little that can be ruined.

Looking to the future

In no time I am sure Jessica will want to decorate her room on her own, but for now I have had great fun organizing things with her advice! My own childhood bedrooms have had such an important influence on me. My love of rosy chintz, eiderdowns and many other things definitely stems from an early age. It will be interesting for me to see what kind of house Jess ends up with when she is grown-up.

children's rooms

Knitted toys

I love these old-fashioned knitted toys. They are often for sale in my local market and make great gifts for new-born babies. The patterns are still available in knitting stores, too, and it is also possible to find great designs for hand-knitted cardigans with motifs such as Scottie dogs. With a little planning, these patterns are easy to convert to knitted pillow covers.

Raffia embroidery

I bought this basket with the embroidery already applied, but raffia embroidery is, in fact, simple to do. Colored raffia is quite easy to come by and simple designs can be quick and effective to create using a blunted embroidery needle with a large eye. I keep a look-out for old handy craft books as they often have good designs in them that are easy to copy.

Cut-outs

As an overall print, this cowboy fabric was rather ugly, but I thought that the emblems themselves would be perfect as cut-outs. When making the appliqué, it is easiest to buy an iron-on backing fabric that holds the material in place before overlocking the edges. I was able to make numerous variations of pillows from one short length of the original fabric.

Ottomans

Old ottomans are great as toy chests. Here I used an old velvet curtain to upholster the sides so that it would better withstand wear and tear. I decided to use the kid's print only for the top so that it will be less expensive to change when Jess grows up and will no doubt want something a little different for her bedroom. Gingham can make a good alternative to plain lining.

the home office

the home office

With the use of computers and modern technology I am able to spend an increasing amount of time working from home. As I commute between my shop and the house, my laptop computer now travels to and fro with me as a regular part of my baggage. I love the peace and quiet of working at home, particularly in the daytime, when I have the space to myself, and often escape from the hustle and bustle of my shop to concentrate on a project at home.

I used to just bring a pile of papers from the office and spread them out over the kitchen table, but I was always short of something, be it a sheet of stationery paper or a stapler. Now, however, with a certain amount of organizing and very little expense I have been able to set up a proper office in the house. The room that I have converted into my workplace is our study. Because it is really an extension of the main living and entertaining room and used by all the family, I needed to retain its domestic atmosphere but somehow incorporate the efficiency of a proper office. The working fireplace has been kept and I use it constantly in the winter, sitting on one of a pair of leather club chairs situated on either side of it. I spend a good deal of time on research, browsing through books and magazines, and I reckon an armchair – if not a sofa – is vital for this. Some simple floor-to-

ceiling book shelves house some of my filing among the books and all in all this gives the room a very cozy atmosphere.

Creating order

I have made two work spaces in the room. One is an old desk with pigeon holes where I keep my mail and paperwork. This tends to get fairly crowded with clutter. Under the desk is the filing system in stacks of box files, each covered in a different paper or fabric. I love mixing all the patterns together rather than having them matching.

Each box is used for a different subject, such as one for bank statements and one for the car documents, and each is instantly recognizable – the yellow stripy box, for example, is for house insurance. Filing like this is so much easier than in a proper filing cabinet as, if information needs to be taken elsewhere, the whole box can be carried around. Clothes pegs instead of paper clips are also good for tidying up paperwork and I keep a huge box of brightly colored plastic pegs on the desk for this purpose.

For messages and notes I have a chalk board, painted red instead of black, propped up above the desk. It is just as practical as a blackboard and much less reminiscent of school. So long as the color is fairly intense to ensure that the chalk is clearly visible, these

OPPOSITE

This desk in the study is normally covered in mounds of paperwork. The 'red board' is a favorite of mine, as is the sculpture of the couple on the bench.

OVERLEAF

A pair of leather armchairs sit on either side of the fireplace. The wire racks (right) are excellent for storing my receipt books and stationery.

boards look great in all sorts of colors. You just need to use an oil-based paint with a matt finish.

I also use an old wire post office rack for my filing and storage. This is excellent for stationery as the wire boxes are exactly the right size for foolscap paper and everything is clearly visible. Although my desk is always cluttered, the sight of all my writing paper and envelopes neatly stacked on the shelves along with the receipt books at least gives the appearance of an efficient work place.

Storage boxes and bags

Cardboard boxes can be a very functional form of storage. I have a pile stacked up by the armchairs. They are full of fabric samples but have somehow ended up doubling as side tables. They are very sturdy with lids and I ordered them from a professional packing and freight company. They come in all sorts of sizes and are incredibly cheap. I have left mine a natural cardboard color but they would look very smart painted or covered in fabric as well.

And then there is my collection of vintage shopping baskets, gathered together over the years. There are many different kinds available, but in particular I look out for the wicker ones with brightly covered plastic handles. They are invaluable for storage all

the home office

Chalk boards

Chalk boards work in all sorts of colors
besides black as long as the shade you choose
is dark enough so that the white writing
shows up on it. It is important, too, to use an
oil-based paint so that the board can be
washed down now and then. It must also
have a flat matt finish or else the chalk will
slip and slide across the surface and the
powder won't adhere especially well.

Vintage fabrics

I love these vintage abstract fabrics but I can
often only find short lengths these days.
They are becoming increasingly collectible so
I am careful not to cut them up to make such
small items as pillow covers or napkins. These
sort of prints can look great once they are
simply framed on a plain canvas stretcher
and hung on the wall alongside
contemporary paintings.

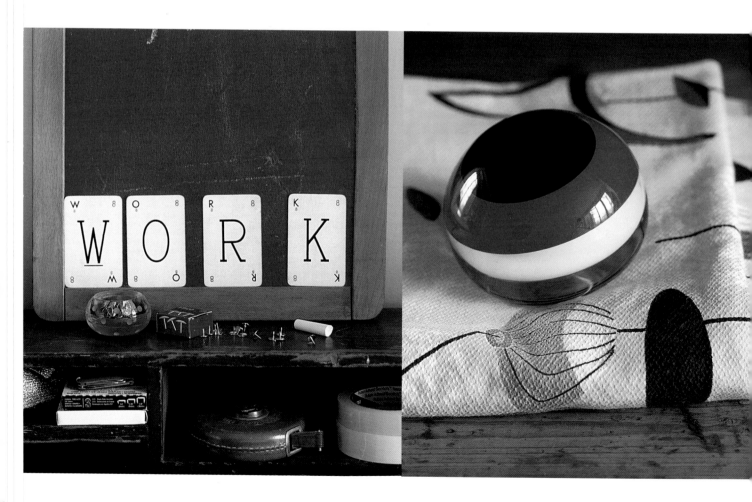

Filing

For filing, I use piles of storage boxes instead of a filing cabinet as they are much more portable when I work between my home and the office. I keep them stacked up under my desk and try to have each one in a different print so that they are easily recognizable. I now know at a glance which is, say, car insurance or the holiday file, and I don't have to search for the label.

Memo board

My memo board has evolved into being a part of my filing system. It is the perfect place to keep my stamps, for example. It began as a plain board but I added the silver foil to brighten it up and then the elastic grid. It is so much more practical to be able to tuck things in behind the tape rather than having to always find a thumbtack. They are never there when you want them.

index

index

author's acknowledgments

So many people have helped me on this project in either a practical way or with their encouragement and support, but in particular I would like to thank Sue Thompson, Angela Vernon, Eva Philipson, Eileen Tyndall, Mrs Noor, Mark Parr and Tony Crawley for all their incredible handywork. Harriet Beauchamp, Jody Kerr, Yvette Masters, Alice Elliot, Sarah Taylor, Nesta Fitzgerald and Gill Hicks for all their support and hard work at the shop. Pia Tryde for her wonderful photographs and for being such an inspiration to work with. Georgina Rhodes, Catherine Bradley, Emma Callery and Denise Bates for all their help, patience and vision. Camilla Lowther, Kevin Kollenda, David Macmillan and Julian Alexander for their help. Jo and Millie for putting up with all the mess when we were working at home. Sarah Landeg who has been the most supportive assistant I could have wished for. Above all, Hugh and Jess for putting up with me while I worked on this project.